Mercury in Dentistry

Preface

Many materials commonly used in dentistry today are considered toxic and harmful to health. Among those materials are the base metals mercury, nickel, lead, chromium, cobalt, beryllium, zinc, tin, copper, and many others. We also apply sterilizing agents such as phenol, formocresol and chlorine directly into root canals. All of the phenols and most of the halogens are considered toxic to some degree.

This profession has a long history with regard to the use of mercury. Although the focus of this presentation is on the heavy metal mercury, the concepts applied can be readily transferred to most of the other dental materials. A recent Louis Harris poll reported that a clean environment is second only to a happy home life among the desires of adults. It is the dentist's responsibility to protect themselves and their staff as well as the patients from exposure to toxic materials.

Most of the technology used by scientists today to uncover hidden environmental hazards was not available even ten years ago. Numerous new illnesses have cropped up from unknown causes, among which environmental exposure to toxics seems to be a most likely suspect. As these investigations continue you can expect to find that many of the most common dental materials will no longer be considered appropriate for use due to their potentially toxic nature.

Modern technology has focused on developing techniques for evaluating biocompatibility that look for minimal damage rather than gross disease. But in the telling words of astronomer Carl Sagan, "Absence of evidence is not evidence of absence."

In this paper I will review the state of the research on the patient's exposure to mercury from dental fillings, the occupational hazards of dentistry, the environmental impact, and how best to protect the dentist, the patients, and the dental staff from injury. This subject has been a source of controversy for over a century. The reason the argument has lasted so long is because investigators did not rely upon the documented scientific literature. Through the use of modern science we can dispel many of the common myths about dental amalgam.

The Chemistry of Mercury

Mercury in Dentistry

Mercury is an unusual base metal that is molten at room temperature. It is highly volatile and vaporizes readily. The fumes from elemental mercury are uncharged atoms (Hg^0) that are easily (75% to 100%) absorbed from lung and nasal tissues[1]. Once absorbed, this uncharged form may enter the bloodstream and penetrate cell membranes, the blood-brain barrier, the placental membrane, and fetal tissues.[2] When combined with the other metals used in a dental amalgam it has the unique property of forming what could be termed a solid suspension. This filling material is not an alloy but rather a mixture. When compressed or heated free vapor mercury will be released.

Mercury combines readily with many compounds, and it has a particular affinity for sulfur. When it attaches to protein molecules, it alters their tertiary structure. This is one way it exerts its poisonous effects. Regardless of the source, once mercury enters the body, the body tries to detoxify the poison. The process of detoxification involves the production of mercurous or mercuric (Hg^+ and Hg^{++}) forms which are not as easily absorbed through cell membranes. Consequently, the biological removal of mercury form tissue is inhibited.

Neurological tissues have a high sulfur content. For this reason, mercury tends to accumulate in the central nervous system.[3] Less than 1 ppm of mercury absorbed into the bloodstream can impair the blood-brain barrier within hours, permitting substances from the plasma that would normally be excluded to enter into the cerebral spinal fluid.[4][5] All mercury compounds appear to cause the same kind of damage in the brain.[6][7][8] Other organs and systems adversely affected by mercury are the immune system, kidneys, liver, and the reproductive and cardiovascular systems. [9][10]

How Does It Poison?

1) Neurological
2) Immunological
3) Endocrine

Because of mercury's effects on the central nervous system, many divergent neurological and psychological symptoms are common findings in mercury

Mercury in Dentistry

poisoning. In 1926 the famous German scientist Dr. Alfred Stock meticulously cataloged and classified these symptoms through conducting experiments on himself. He identified confusion, memory loss, and irritability as associated with inhaling a single 10 ppm dose of mercury. He termed these symptoms *micro-mercurialism.*.[11] Mercury is also associated with depression, suicidal thoughts, nervousness, fits of anger, shyness, and emotional outbursts.

In addition to the psychological symptoms associated with exposure to low doses of mercury, the immune system appears particularly sensitive to this toxin as well. It responds to mercury with an antigen/antibody reaction in an attempt to remove the foreign substance. Two types of white blood cells are involved. T-cells are endowed with special qualities that allow them to migrate to sites of infection and defend against invading microorganisms, viruses, and toxins. B-cells produce antibodies specific for the unwanted invader or foreign substance, which circulate in the plasma.

The immune system's response works like this. When T-cells recognize the presence of an antigen, they stimulate the B-cells (memory cells) to produce antibodies to the antigen. The B-cells, along with a special class of T-cells called helper cells, then surround and engulf the antigen and neutralize it. Once the job is complete, other T-cells (suppressors) suppress further production of antibodies. The used-up B-cells, along with the antibodies and toxins or dead germs, are excreted through the kidneys and feces. An allergic reaction is similar, except that the B-cell antibodies also cause a release of histamines. Histamines are what causes the tissue breakdown and red skin reaction.

White blood cells are very sensitive to mercury exposure and as a result, their numbers at first increase and later, as they die, the numbers will decrease. Other toxic effects on the white blood cells also result from exposure to mercury. Release of the migratory inhibitory factor appears reduced, and antinuclear antibodies are formed, so that the immune system appears to attack itself. And the respiratory burst of the white blood cells (the mechanism by which white blood cells attack bacterial invaders) is inhibited.[12] Exposure to mercury causes the chromosomes of white blood cells to break and form unusual combinations and genetic aberrations.[13][14][15] White blood cells from mercury-diseased rats show a significant decrease in ability to replicate their own chromosomes, and 90% of the cells develop autoimmune antibodies for their own nuclei.[16][17] Mercury also suppresses the primary humeral antibody response.[18][19][20][21][22]

In a preliminary study Dr. David Eggleston demonstrated that both mercury and nickel dental restorations suppress the quantity of circulating T-cells present in humans.[23] Vera Stejfkal, M.D. of Sweden has documented the immunological response to mercury in humans. She has even found an adverse reaction in infants when a mercury preservative (thimerosal) is used with the inoculum. While further research is badly needed in this new area of science, it is clear that mercury plays a very important role in immunosuppression. Its adverse effects on human resistance to diseases and tumors cannot be overlooked.[24]

The endocrine system is also affected by the accumulation of mercury in certain critical tissues. Not only does inhalation of this volatile substance allow transport from the lungs into the bloodstream. In addition, the nasal mucosa can apparently transport it directly to the brain and pituitary. It is here that critical hormone balances can be damaged. (See Reproductive Defects)

How Toxic Is Mercury Compared to Other Metallic Compounds?

To answer this question, Sharma and associates studied the cytotoxic effects of several compounds on chick ganglia. They stated in their conclusions: *Our study showed mercury, cadmium, and lead in decreasing order of toxicity.*[25]

SEVERELY TOXIC	MODERATELY TOXIC	SLIGHTLY TOXIC
MERCURY	THALLIUM	LEAD
CADMIUM	ARSENIC	ARSENIC
ARSENIC	SELENIUM	TIN OXIDE
VANDEX-TIN	COPPER	

Industrial Exposure

In order to protect workers from excessive exposure to toxic materials, the governments of all the developed nations and the World Health Organization (WHO) have adopted adult industrial standards for mercury exposure. In addition to these industrial exposure standards, many governments have also enacted

Mercury in Dentistry

legislation called environmental standards, or simply EPA, to protect the general populace from excessive pollution.

Environmental standards are strictly enforced in California, and our state government at the request of the people has placed even more stringent requirements on many emissions than the federal government has. In the United States the U.S. EPA standard is the only non-occupational standard, and as a result it is the only exposure considered appropriate for the majority of the population. When looking at the question of toxins in dental restorations, it is reasonable to conclude that restorations should certainly not increase the patients' exposure to levels of toxic materials that exceed the EPA health standards. Beyond that, it should be noted that both the U.S. EPA and WHO have stated that no amount of exposure to mercury can be considered totally harmless, and it is not possible to establish a level at which no response will be seen.[26]

Some individuals in society are at higher risk from toxic exposure than others. Such groups include the elderly, pregnant women, women of childbearing age (for possible unsuspected or near future pregnancy), infants, children, the hypersensitive, immunosuppressed, and those already occupationally exposed. The Occupational Safety and Health Act (OSHA) has recommended no exposure of fertile women to amounts of mercury greater than 10 micrograms per cubic meter of air, and **pregnant women should be occupationally exposed to no mercury.**

Individual Intra-oral Exposure

Although evidence that mercury was leaking from dental fillings was previously discovered in 1926 by the aforementioned Dr. Alfred Stock, and again noted in 1979,[27] in 1981 Dr. Carl Svare[28] partly by chance made a rediscovery that shocked the dental community. To conduct a series of experiments on the amount of mercury in expired air, he had asked for volunteers from among his dental students. One woman waiting at the end of the line saw that it would be some time before she was to be tested. So she went across the street the have a pizza for lunch. When she returned, the line was gone and Dr. Svare tested the mercury in her exhaled breath. Her mercury measurement was so high it blew out his equipment.

Mercury in Dentistry

When he learned that she had just eaten a pizza, he recovered some of the uneaten pizza and could find no mercury contamination. With further experimentation, Dr. Svare noted that the student's mercury vapor level began to drop. He then gave her a piece of rubber tubing and instructed her to chew on it for a while. He was amazed: her mercury level shot right back up. The other students were recalled and re-measured after chewing sugarless gum with similar results. This landmark study became known as the Chewing Gum Study. It led to subsequent findings that mercury release from fillings increases dramatically by 15-fold whenever the fillings are stimulated by chewing, brushing, hot fluids, bruxism, etc. Numerous other investigators have confirmed these results.[29] [30] [31] [32] [33]

Low doses of mercury are almost completely absorbed from the lungs before exhaling. Therefore, Dr. Svare's exhaled air measurements represent only a small fraction of the dose absorbed by an individual. We also know that personal habits such as night grinding, gum chewing, and mouth breathing can greatly affect the rate of release of mercury from fillings. Because of wide variations in such personal habits, it is not possible with present technology to predict which patients will release the most mercury. But an average daily dose can be estimated.

In 1985 Dr. Murray Vimy, et al. took the examination several steps further by subjecting the chewing to a standardization technique and plotting the increase of mercury release with respect to time.[34] [35] He discovered that fillings take only 10 minutes to reach maximum output and do not immediately stop releasing when chewing stops, but rather continue for a period of up to 90 minutes. This was termed the "cool down" period.

He then began the extremely complicated process of estimating how much mercury a person might absorb daily from mercury fillings. For the conversion from intra-oral air exposure to absorbed intake, consideration was given to such factors as respiratory volume, absorption rate, oral-nasal breathing ratio, frequency and duration of chewing, and cool down period following stimulation. In each instance the lowest possible estimate was chosen to avoid overestimating the risk posed by the release of mercury from fillings. Vimy concluded that by the most conservative estimate, the average person with 12 fillings would absorb approximately 11 micrograms per day from the fillings alone.[36] [37]

To put this estimate in perspective I have prepared the following graph. It compares the EPA maximum daily dose of mercury from: sources other than air,

Mercury in Dentistry

air alone(i.e. smog), and all sources combined. Note that the EPA standard is based on an adult weight of 165 lb (75 kg). To be applicable to small children, it should be reduced in proportion to their weight.

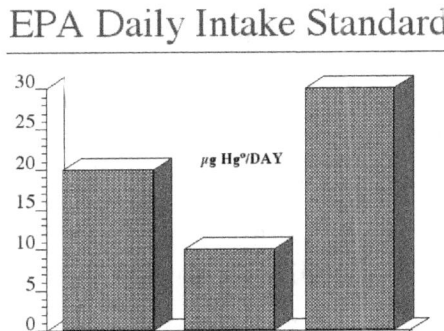

EPA Daily Intake Standard

The most obvious result of mercury/silver dental implants is an increase in the individual's exposure to mercury. This is demonstrated by elevated blood levels that are measurably higher for those with fillings than those without.[38] The following graph shows the findings of three different researchers measuring intra-oral mercury vapor.

In his reports, Vimy stressed the concept of "average intake" to allow for the fact that some of the people examined were definitely not average. For example, Dr. Svare's young dental student was well over 100 $\mu g/m^3$, where the average person was measured at 32 $\mu g/m^3$. Thus, the daily intake for this young woman would be 3 times 11 or 33 μg of Hg per day.

Sellers discovered an even more disturbing phenomenon. His experiment involved children aged 11 to 13 with mixed dentition. Of the children with amalgams, Sellers found 33% with intra-oral levels above 50 $\mu g/m^3$.[39] In fact, 47% of the children who had 6 fillings or more tested above 50 $\mu g/m^3$. Sellers failed to fully appreciate the seriousness of such high exposure levels, however. He commented that "*Such concentration may not be any more dangerous than briefly walking through a contaminated workplace* --an interpretation revealing an apparent disregard for the safety of children. (It is of interest to note that Sellers denies writing these words and contends that the conclusions of his article were changed after submission to the Texas Dental Journal[40])

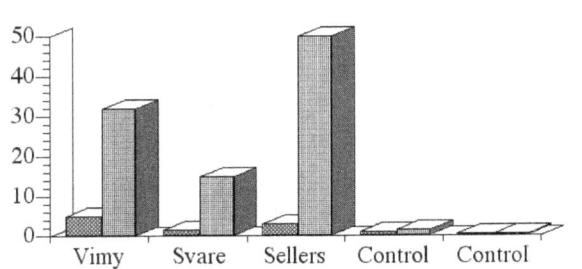

Intra-Oral Mercury Vapor

Mercury in Dentistry

In my opinion, the most important feature of this study is that it clearly demonstrated children with fewer teeth and fillings rapidly reach higher mercury vapor levels than adults.

It is important to keep in mind that the industrial standard is not an environmental standard and was never meant to protect the health of children. Rather, it is clearly a workplace standard meant for consenting adults who work 40 hours a week and are medically monitored. They are presumably paid a salary commensurate with the obvious risks to which they are exposed.

It is the policy of the State of California to destroy school buildings that cannot achieve compliance with the EPA standards. It is unlikely that any informed parents would give their children permission to play in a toxic waste dump 4 to 10 or more hours daily. Should toxic poisons be placed in their mouths instead?

Sellers' experiment is further flawed since the chewing terminated after only 4 minutes and therefore did not allow the children to chew for the full 10 minutes necessary to maximally stimulate the fillings. Vimy's previous research had demonstrated that the dramatic increase in output continues to rise for 10 minutes. One can only speculate the levels that would have been achieved had the author allowed the children to reach maximum output. In the United States today many children chew gum all day. It is clear from the discussion that the author failed to recognize the inherent medical, legal, and moral liabilities of exposing the children to such high levels of this toxic material.

Abraham, et al. provided additional information regarding blood levels and the release of mercury from fillings. In their experiment, baseline blood and breath air samples were taken after subjects had not eaten or drunk anything for the previous 12 hours. Then the subjects were required to chew gum for three minutes at 120 beats per minute, followed by post-chewing blood and breath air samples.

Subjects with amalgam measured higher both before and after chewing than those without, and there was no change in the no-amalgam group following chewing. Those with amalgam fillings measured post-chewing levels higher than prechewing levels in both blood and breath. Abraham, et al. concluded their report by stating: *Given these facts, the small increase in blood mercury levels that is statistically associated with dental amalgam restorations should be a matter of concern for dentists as well as for the recipients of these restorations.*[41]

Mercury in Dentistry

It should again be pointed out here that three minutes of chewing does not correspond to normal chewing and would not have allowed the fillings to reach their maximum output.

Previous studies by Kroncke, et al. and Ott and Kroncke[42][43] had failed to find a connection between blood levels and the *number* of amalgam fillings, although they did find that those with amalgam had higher blood levels than those without. Their work has not been verified by other investigators, and the preponderance of scientific data suggests that they failed to find correctly.[44] There is also a question about their sampling technique, which may have caused the loss of mercury from their samples. In addition, blood alcohol was not recorded. Alcohol will greatly reduce blood levels and perhaps increase tissue levels. Their experimental group may also have had some additional external exposure to mercury.

Does Dental Amalgam Contribute Significantly to the Body Burden?

One way to evaluate this question is to analyze human autopsy tissues for mercury accumulation. Till sectioned tissues and human jawbone around teeth with and without amalgam fillings and found high levels of mercury around teeth with fillings. Surprisingly he found even greater amounts if a gold crown covered an amalgam.[45]

The biological half-life of mercury in human nervous tissues appears to be over 10,000 days (27 years).[46][47] Since the brain is sensitive to mercury, many of the first symptoms of mercury poisoning are neurological and psychological in nature. The action of mercury on the brain may occur by blocking the metabolism in nerve tissue which frequently causes irreversible damage.[48]

Certain areas in the brain tend to collect much more mercury than others. The pituitary gland which regulates the human hormonal system preferentially collects mercury at a rate 10 times greater than the brain as a whole.[49] It is also well recognized that mercury has an adverse effect on fetal neurological development.

It can be assumed that if mercury is present and the source is amalgam fillings, then autopsy tissue samples taken from individuals with amalgam fillings would contain more mercury than samples from those without fillings. In one of

Mercury in Dentistry

the largest human autopsy studies conducted so far, University of Southern California professor Dr. David Eggleston performed over 100 human brain biopsies and analyzed them for mercury. The results showed a high positive correlation between the amount of mercury in the brain and the size and number of fillings in the mouth. The experiment found a 3- to 4-fold greater occipital lobe brain burden of mercury for those with an average number of fillings than for those without fillings.

These results are also particularly significant because they confirm earlier studies and show unquestionably that dental mercury does escape from fillings, is absorbed, and does contribute significantly to the total body burden of mercury.[50]

The U.S. EPA has established the optimum intake of mercury is 0 μg/day! They have suggested that 30 micrograms is the maximum allowable daily dose of mercury from all sources, with just 10 of these μg allocated to sources other than air. All sources and forms of mercury are considered equal and cumulative.

WHO expert committee calculated that the human daily dose of mercury from various sources is:

Dental amalgam	= 3.0-17.0 μg/day (Hg vapor)
Fish and seafood	= 2.3 μg/day (methylmercury)
Other food	= 0.3 μg/day (inorganic Hg)
Air & water	= Negligible traces

The WHO also noted that "**A specific No-Observed--Effect Level (NOEL) for mercury cannot be established.**"[51] In other words, because the effects of mercury poisoning are cumulative and long-term, the only definitely safe exposure is no exposure at all. We can now definitely state that as a direct and persistent result of amalgam implants the patient's immune system is altered, gingival tissues and jawbone adjacent to the tooth are saturated with mercury, and the mercury content of the brain increases by three- to fourfold. And as a result of extensive use of this material, silver/mercury fillings are now considered by the World Health Organization to be the predominant source of human exposure.[52] [53]

Mercury in Dentistry

In 1987 an expert committee instructed to review the safety of dental amalgam by the Swedish Socialstyrelsen (Department of Health) concluded that *from a toxicological point of view, mercury is too toxic for use as a filling material and dentists should use other materials as soon as they are available. As a first step amalgam work on women who are pregnant should cease because of danger of damage to the brain of the fetus.*[54]

Dentists and Personnel Exposure

While the issue of patient exposure is still the subject of intense investigation, there is no question that dentists are at risk. Let me preface my remarks regarding the urinary excretion of mercury in dental personnel by quoting a short excerpt from Goldwater, et al.: *Urinary mercury levels may give some indication of the degree of exposure. They are of limited value in the diagnosis of poisoning, since high levels can be found in human subjects who are symptom-free, and low levels in those exhibiting marked evidence of mercurialism. It has been suggested that, in some cases, failure to excrete mercury is a factor in the development of poisoning. Those investigators who have studied the subject are in almost unanimous agreement that there is poor correlation between the urinary excretion of mercury and the occurrence of demonstrable evidence of poisoning.*[55] [56]

Urinary excretion may, however, provide some information on a group basis as to degree of exposure. This has been publicly acknowledged at the National Institute of Dental Research (NIDR) workshop on the biocompatibility of metals in dentistry.[57]

As part of the ADA's Health Assessment Program held at ADA annual sessions in the years 1975 through 1983, the urinary mercury levels of 4,272 U.S. dentists were measured. The mean level was 14.2 micrograms/liter with a range from 0 to 556 micrograms/liter. An increase in the mean mercury level was found to be correlated with increase in age of the office, the practice, and the dentist. The highest mean was found in general dentists, at 15.3 μg/l, and the lowest was found in orthodontists, at 3.9 μg/l. Blood samples of 1,555 dentists found that the mean for all dentists was 8.2 ng Hg/ml blood, and the mean for general dentists was 8.8

Mercury in Dentistry

ng Hg/ml.[58]

times greater
blood level
Abraham
with

    In the
urine level
population is
above 20
abnormal. 4
considered

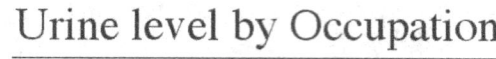

Urine level by Occupation

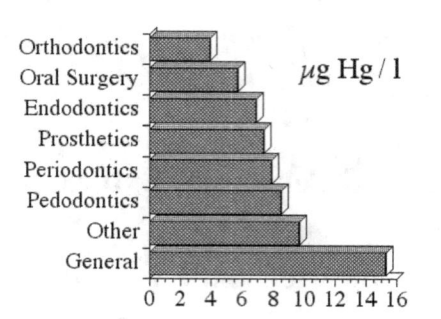

μg Hg / l

That is
approximately 12
than the mean
of 0.7 ng/ml
found for those
fillings.[59]
U.S. the average
for the general
0 to 5 μg/l, with
μg/l considered
μg Hg/l is
excessive in the

Federal Republic of Germany.[60] The U.S. Center for Disease Control has published the opinion that 30 μg Hg/l urine is the maximum accepted level. 50 μg/l is associated with load-induced tremors, and 100 μg/l is generally associated with outright tremors.[61] Furthermore, a study by Berlin showed that inhalation of mercury vapor selectively increased the uptake in the brain.[62] The recent animal study by Vimy shows why there is no blood or urine threshold for mercury which can be considered totally safe. In Vimy's sheep study, the blood levels remained low and urine level never exceeded 10 ng Hg/g, yet high levels of mercury were found accumulated in critical organs.[63]

    In their report on the Biocompatibility of Metals in Dentistry, the NIDR published the opinion that *The distribution of mercury into body tissues is highly variable and appears to be of little correlation between levels in urine, blood, or hair and toxic effects.* On the other hand, high urinary output on a group basis may indeed indicate high exposure. If exposure is prolonged, then urinary levels will eventually drop as the kidneys lose their ability to remove mercury from the blood.

    In summary, then, since the ADA Health Assessment Program's studies of dentists and dental personnel found urinary output 3 to 15 times that of the general population,[64] there seems to be little question that we are excessively exposed. The following percentages reveal the extent of that overexposure.

19.1% measured over 20 μg/Hg/l	(29,500 U.S. dentists)
10.9% measured over 30 μg/Hg/l	(16,500 U.S. dentists)

Mercury in Dentistry

4.9% measured over 50 μg/Hg/l	(7,500 U.S. dentists)
1.3% measured over 100 μg/Hg/l	(2,000 U.S. dentists)

For the last 20 years dental offices have been tested for compliance with various industrial standards. In addition, several statistical surveys of dentist's exposure levels have been conducted. Dentist's offices do not fare too well when compared to these safety standards. As you may have noted, the U.S. has one of the highest exposure standards in the world. Despite this, over 10% of dentist's dental offices exceed this standard. A 1983 survey of British dental offices found that 10% of those also violated that country's industrial exposure standard of 50 μg/Hg time-weighted average (TWA).[65]

Dental Offices over 50 TLV

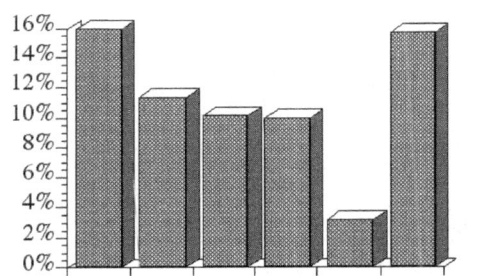

Many procedures common to the practice of dentistry are known to release mercury vapor. Such routine duties as condensing, polishing, grinding, and mixing amalgam will send an invisible shower of mercury droplets into the air.[66] These droplets may be inhaled or may fall to the floor and vaporize. Dental offices have been studied extensively in the scientific literature to see how the handling of mercury affects the ambient level of mercury vapor found in the workplace. Theoretically, the type of flooring should make a difference. However, this did not seem to be one of the critical factors.[67][68] Research indicates that the process of mixing, packing, drilling, and polishing a mercury/silver filling will expose everyone present to high levels of mercury.[69][70][71][72][73][74][75] i

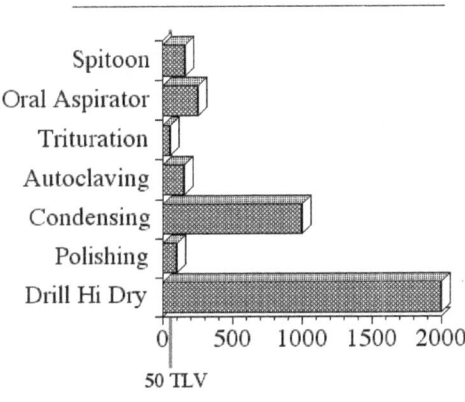

In his lecture at Tuffs in Boston, Mass., Dr. Patrick

Mercury in Dentistry

Störtebecker discussed the <u>Direct Transport of Mercury from the Oronasal Cavity to the Cranial Cavity as a Cause of Dental Amalgam Poisoning</u> .[76] He further discussed the valveless venous passage of mercury into the pituitary and other areas of the brain from the nasal passages in his book <u>Silver Mercury Fillings: A Hazard to the Human Brain</u>.[77] Störtebecker confirmed his theory of the nasal pathway through conducting experiments with dogs.[78] The dogs were sacrificed soon after inhaling low levels of mercury vapor. The graph demonstrates the ability of the brain to selectively accumulate mercury. Those areas closer to the nasal passages had considerably more mercury than the areas farthest away.

In an earlier experiment, Dr. Alfred Stock had studied the transport of mercury to the brain via the nasal mucosa by applying a mercury-containing ointment to the nasal mucous

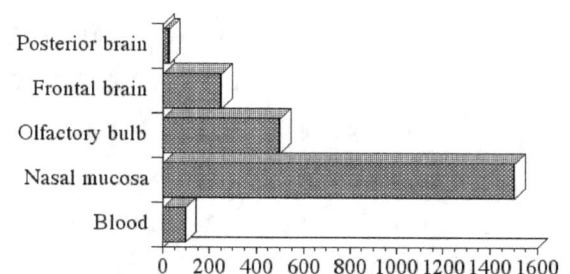

Störtebecker: Swedish J. Biol Med 89

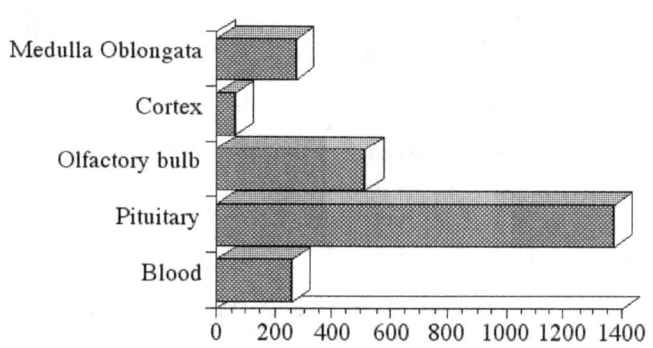

Dr. Alfred Stock

membrane during the final hours of a terminal cancer patient's life. Postmortem examination for mercury content revealed a considerable accumulation in that short time in both the pituitary and frontal brain.

Dr. Stock concluded that the high concentration of mercury in the pituitary was best explained by the assumption that it was transported there from the olfactory bulbs, since they too contained a larger quantity of mercury.[79] (While such types of experiments may be criticized by today's standards, they were considered the norm at that time. Still, the information they provided was virtually

Mercury in Dentistry

ignored for 50 years until a young Swedish scientist, Magnus Nylander, D.D.S., devised a way to study dentists.)

Our present level of exposure to mercury is associated with many health problems, most notably birth defects and neurological disorders.[80][81][82][83][84] A 1987 study by Sikorski identified a significant positive correlation between mercury levels in the hair of occupationally exposed women and the occurrence of reproductive failures and menstrual cycle disorders.[85] Recently reported in the literature is the case of a young dentist, professionally exposed to mercury for 35 weeks during her pregnancy, who delivered a severely brain-damaged infant.[86] Could this tragic outcome possibly have been prevented if dentists were more aware of the hazards of mercury poisoning in their practices?

The authors of the textbook Occupational Hazards in the Health Professions cautioned against comprehensive amalgam work during pregnancy.[87] Koos and Lango stated as early as 1970 that their research indicated that fertile women should be exposed to no more than 10 Hg $\mu g/m^3$, and pregnant women should be exposed to no mercury at all.[88]

In this modern day when most offices have several mechanical mixers, exposure seems to be increasing nevertheless. Some authors have felt that the type of amalgam capsule is of critical importance.[89] Precapsulated mixes appeared to reduce exposure if handled properly.[90] Other investigators have found no correlation between the care with which mercury is handled and exposure levels.[91]

It is likely that the use of this material makes exposure inevitable.[92] Furthermore, at present no known procedure will permit this material to be implanted in the mouth and still keep the patient's breath within the EPA standards for the air.

Clearly, women in dentistry are at the greatest risk from exposure to this toxic substance. One assistant's death has been reported.[93] The United States Environmental Protection Agency states that *Women chronically exposed to mercury vapor experience increased frequency of menstrual disturbances and spontaneous abortions; also a high mortality rate was observed among infants born to women who displayed symptoms of mercury poisoning.*[94] It would be interesting, then, to examine the literature for evidence that dentists and dental personnel are absorbing higher than normal amounts of mercury.

Mercury in Dentistry

Dental Personnel Health Risks

The kidney filters the blood, and as a result chronic exposure to chemicals might eventually induce kidney damage. A 1988 study by Verschoor, et al. evaluated the kidney function of 68 dentists (63 men, 5 women) and 64 female assistants who were apparently healthy, not pregnant, and taking no drugs. They compared the results of their kidney function analysis to 250 workers known to be exposed through the workplace to lead, cadmium, or chromium. Their conclusion was that *Dentists and dental assistants appear to have a higher potential risk of kidney function disturbances than the workers in these industries. Although this study did not present evidence for changes of renal function parameters in dental practice in relation to Hg-urine levels below 20 µg/l, it certainly suggests that dental practice may carry a risk of renal dysfunction. There is a need to assess the renal hazard of the potential nephrotoxic chemicals used in dental practice.*[95]

Kuntz followed 57 prenatal patients with no known exposure to mercury for changes in whole blood from initial prenatal examination to delivery and postpartum hospitalization. The mothers' whole blood total mercury increased during pregnancy from .79 ppb at initial examination to 1.16 ppb at delivery. This represents a 46% increase during pregnancy. Mercury has previously been recognized for its particular ease of crossing the placental membrane. The umbilical cord blood was also sampled at birth and found to have even higher levels of mercury at 1.5 ppb.[96] After careful analysis of the data, Kuntz concluded: *Previous stillbirths, as well as history of birth defects, exhibited significant positive correlation with background mercury levels.* He further stated that patients with large numbers of dental fillings exhibited a tendency to higher maternal blood levels, which agrees with both Ott and Abraham.[97]

Vimy has confirmed the transport of mercury from fillings to the fetus in experimental animals (sheep and monkey) and the additional exposure through mothers milk.[98] Berlin has shown the fetal blood content of mercury was raised dramatically at the end of pregnancy exceeding that of the mother at delivery by a factor of at least five. Early abortion, premature birth, low birth weight with a perinatal death have been observed in monkeys.[99]

Mercury in Dentistry

A criticism of the earlier Kuntz study is that the levels of mercury found were too close to the controls to conclude without further study that a definite correlation with stillbirths had in fact been proven to exist.

Women Exposed to Mercury Vapor Have a Higher Incidence of Menstrual Disturbances

Mikhailova, et al. found that 26.8% of women working in a mercury polluted atmosphere suffered from menstrual disturbances. Marinova, et al. found that 29% had hypermenorrhea.[100] The controls found only 0.3% with the same condition. Hypomenorrhea occurred in 15.3% of the exposed group and only 0.6% of the nonexposed group. This could mean that more than 44% of female dental personnel working under these conditions will suffer from reproductive disorders due to mercury in the dental office. This hypothesis is corroborated by two other studies of women occupationally exposed to mercury which found that 36% to 45% will develop these types of disorders within 6 months of employment, a proportion that increases to 67% within 3 years of employment.[101 102]

This hypothesis has been further confirmed a recent study of 418 women working in dentistry who became pregnant during the previous four years. Detailed information was collected on mercury handling practices and the number of non-contraception menstrual cycles it took the women to become pregnant. Dental assistants not working with amalgam served as unexposed controls. Women working in offices with poor mercury hygiene factors took longer to become pregnant. The fecundability (probability of conceiving in any given menstrual cycle) of this high exposure group was only 50% of that for unexposed women after controlling for age, smoking, race, frequency of intercourse, history of pelvic inflammatory disease, year the attempt began, and occupational exposure to cold sterilants, x-rays, and unscavanged nitrous oxide. No relationship was found between the number of amalgam surfaces and in a woman's own mouth and her fertility. Unfortunately no intra-oral assessment of mercury exposure was made.[103]

Mercury in Dentistry

The most common symptoms were dysmenorrhea (painful menstruation), hypermenorrhea, anovulation (infertility >40%), and hypomenorrhea. These symptoms are known to increase in populations additionally exposed to lead.[104] The relationship between spontaneous abortion, stillborn infants, and mercury has also been confirmed.[105]

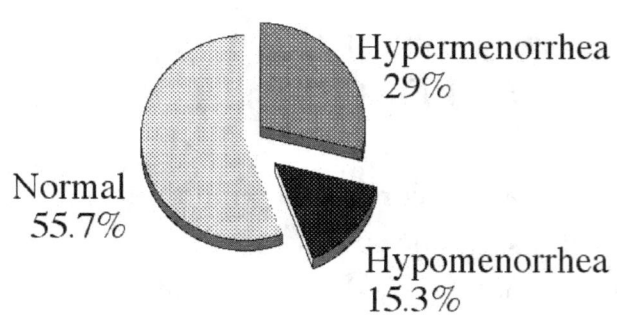

Marinova et al mercury exposed

Hypermenorrhea 29%

Normal 55.7%

Hypomenorrhea 15.3%

Problems that may develop in the fetus from maternal exposure are not always evident at birth. Prenatal exposure to mercury vapor has been shown to have an effect on brain development.[106] Such delayed problems include diminished learning capacity, muscle spasms, and altered electroencephalograms.[107] Exposure continues to increase if the infant is nursed, since mercury concentrates 8 fold in breast milk.[108] [109]

Proper Handling of Amalgam

The ADA and others have repeatedly pointed out that dentists are exposed to large amounts of mercury both in school during their training and in their profession through the use of this restorative material. In addition, mixed dental amalgam has been ruled a hazardous substance by the U.S. EPA. Specific instructions in the disposal and handling of dental amalgam have been given.[110] [111] [112]

1) A no-touch technique of handling amalgam should be used. Direct contact or handling of mercury, amalgam, or other mercury-containing materials should be avoided.

2) All amalgam scraps should be salvaged and stored in a tightly closed container. They should be covered with a sulfide solution such as X-ray fixer solution.

3) Skin exposed to mercury should be washed thoroughly.

4) Precapsulated alloy should be used, and used capsules resealed.

Mercury in Dentistry

5)   Water and high-volume evacuation should always be used, both when removing old fillings and when finishing new restorations. Evacuation systems should be passed through filters, strainers, or traps, and not exhausted into the office or directly into the sewer.

6)   A face mask should be used to avoid breathing amalgam dust.

7)   The dental office should be monitored for mercury vapor once a year or more often if contamination is suspected.

8)   Periodic urinalysis of all dental personnel should be conducted.

Unfortunately these steps are insufficient since they do not protect the patient or the dentist and the dental staff from elemental mercury vapor and respirable particles that are created when amalgams are manipulated with high-speed drills and diamonds since the mask that they wear does not protect against either.

Many skeptics maintain that if mercury were as dangerous a poison as numerous medical, environmental, occupational, health, and safety agencies have concluded, then there should be overt symptoms of mercury poisoning in the dental profession. Although that is not a very scientifically valid approach, it appears to be a reasonable hypothesis. The next area we will examine, then, will be additional evidence of mercury poisoning and related injuries in the dental profession.

Allergy/Hypersensitivity

Some authorities believe that mercury/silver fillings are not a problem except for the rare individual who is hypersensitive to mercury.[113] There is no scientific evidence to support this contention. However, assuming that it were true for the general public, it would also be true for dental personnel.

A hypersensitive response is an abnormal immune reaction to an allergen. Mercury is an allergen. Numerous health problems have been related to allergic reactions to mercury. Idiosyncratic responses to metallic mercury have been documented since the last century. In 1943 Bass submitted a case report of urticaria response in a child after receiving dental amalgam fillings.[114] Also documented in the scientific literature are chronic atrophic dermatitis[115], contact dermatitis[116 117 118 119], eczematous dermatitis[120], multiple polyposis[121], generalized allergic reactions[122 123 124 125], oral lichens planus (62% of those with lichens planus tested allergic)[126 127 128 129], chronic oral ulcerations[130], and burning mouth[131].

Two studies have examined the risk of hypersensitivity to inorganic mercury in dental personnel. The first tests were by White and Brandt, who patch tested dental students with mercuric chloride and silver amalgam to determine their hypersensitivity.[132] As you can see by the table, freshmen tested lower than seniors in mercury hypersensitivity. The study concluded that exposure during training in dental school could lead to increased hypersensitivity response in students.

A more recent study by Miller, et al. found an increase in hypersensitivity corresponding not with years in school, but rather with increasing number and age of the subjects' amalgam restorations.[133] Overall, they found an even greater percentage of the 171 dental student participants who tested allergic/hypersensitive to mercury.

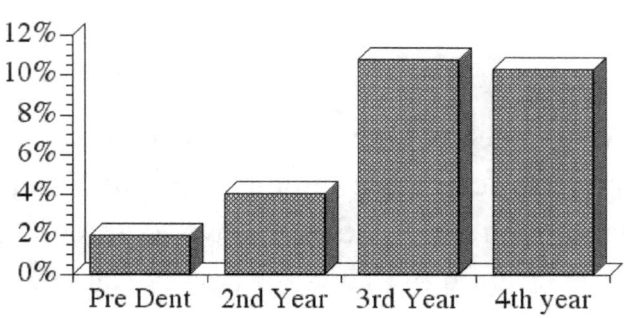

White and Brandt 1976

Miller's study considered freshmen dental students to be representative of the general public. He found that 31.4% of freshmen tested positive to mercuric chloride.

Djerassi also tested for allergy and found that of those with amalgams, 16.1% tested allergic, whereas none of the 60 control subjects without amalgams tested allergic.[134]

Neuman, a dental professor and spokesperson for the ADA, contended at the California Dental Association meeting in 1987 that the positive patch test is actually a chemical burn and is not related to mercury hypersensitivity.[135] The

Miller et. al. 1985

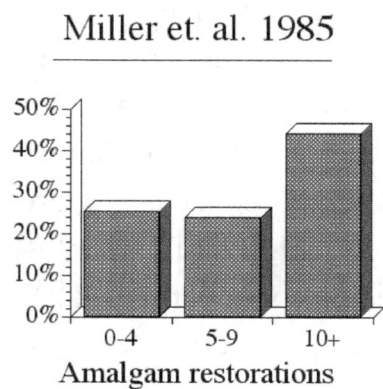

Amalgam restorations

protocol of this and other studies has precluded that possibility. The negative controls for both the Miller study and the Djerassi study found that 0% of those who had no fillings tested positive for hypersensitivity. (As an interesting side note, in California it is against the law for tattoo artists to use red dye in their designs, because it contains mercury. There are reported cases of the development of hypersensitivity to dental fillings after placement of a red tattoo.[136])

Miller concluded that hypersensitivity is apparently related to subjects' number of amalgam fillings and the length of time they have been in place, rather than to the number of years spent in the dental profession. The risk of developing an abnormal response increases with both time worn and number of fillings. Contact dermatitis has indeed forced a number of dentists out of practice, since they could no longer wear gloves or handle amalgam. It is considered an occupational hazard, with approximately 11% of all dentists displaying an allergic hypersensitivity reaction to gloves.[137]

Neurological Damage

In a study of 298 dentists, Shapiro measured their mercury levels by X-ray fluorescence. Of those dentists with greater than 20 μg Hg/liter tissue levels, 30% had polyneuropathies, while those dentists with no detectable mercury levels had no polyneuropathies. Shapiro concluded that these findings suggest that the use of mercury as a restorative material is a health risk for dentists.[138]

Dr. Magnus Nylander devised a series of experiments utilizing neutron activation analysis (NAA) to study the mercury content of brain tissues of amalgam bearers, non-amalgam bearers, and dentists. NAA was the most accurate method currently known to science at that time to evaluate trace minerals. What he found in the cases of 7 dentists and 1 dental nurse was that all had a surprisingly high pituitary mercury content, totally out of proportion to the content found in other parts of the brain. Values ranged from 135 to 4,000 nanograms Hg per gram tissue.[139] [140] He also found in a related study of dentists and dental assistants in Sweden that they have twice the incidence of brain tumors as non-dental personnel.[141]

Table

Mercury in Dentistry

	Pituitary	Occipital	Ratio
1) Dentist	4,040	300	14:1
2) Dentist	3,650	84	43:1
3) Dentist	2,700	16	169:1
4) Dentist	350	40	9:1
5) Dentist	350	5	70:1
6) Dentist	350	17	18:1
7) Dentist	135	19	7:1
8) Assistant	1300	18	72:1
Amalgam bearers	7-77	3-23	
Cases 9-23 Mean	28	11	2.5:1
24)	10	6	2:1
25)	5	6	1:1

The evidence is clear that dentists are exposing themselves, their staff and their patients to a known toxic material through the use of mercury in dentistry. One of the principal reasons this has happened is the strong advocacy position of the American Dental Association in support of the use of this material.

The ADA was formed in 1859 by mercury-placing dentists to support their belief that mercury fillings were safe. In the last 132 years the organization has championed the cause of mercury fillings and its spokesmen have on many occasions made numerous statements proclaiming amalgam's safety. The most recent and comprehensive article appeared in the April 1990 issue of the Journal of the American Dental Association.

In response to the numerous false and misleading statements contained in that article the International Academy of Oral Medicine and Toxicology prepared a scientifically documented response. That paper is still today the most complete scientific review of the myths and falsehoods regarding the use of dental amalgam. For your further information it is available for download from Saveteeth.org and on the web sight of the International Academy of Oral Medicine and Toxicology at www.IAOMT.org.

Mercury in Dentistry

Responsibility

Who is responsible?

The American Dental Association in 1992 declared their position in response to a lawsuit (Tollhurst vs. ADA). Their attorneys pleaded: **"The ADA has no legal duty of care to protect the public from allegedly harmful dental materials. The ADA did not manufacture, distribute or install the amalgam fillings."** The judge agreed and dismissed the ADA as a defendant in the case.

The use of amalgam is contraindicated;

* In proximal or occlusal contact to dissimilar metal restorations.
* In patients with severe renal deficiency
* In patients with known allergies to amalgam
* For retrograde or endodontic filling
* As a filling material for cast crown
* In children 6 and under
* In expectant mothers.

Dentsply Caulk has informed the dental profession in their Material Safety Data Sheet for Dispersalloy,[142] one of the most popular high copper dental amalgams, of the contraindications for amalgam use. Their warnings are dramatically different from the procedures commonly taught in dental schools, found in many dental practices and as advocated by the ADA. This information certainly can be used in court to deflect liability suits away from the manufacturers toward the dentist.

California, after arguing in court for over 10 years with the California Dental Association, has won and now requires that dental clinics with 10 or more employees inform patients who might be exposed to mercury that, **"Dental amalgams contain mercury. Mercury is known to the State of California to cause fetal brain damage, infertility and birth defects".**

It is clear that few if any mercury-placing dentist give accurate informed consent or full disclosure to their patients prior to implanting this time-release mercury filling.

The United States Food and Drug Administration has defined an implant as, **"any substance implanted into a natural or man made body cavity."** The ADA asked for amalgam to be exempted from this definition. The FDA refused. By law manufacturer must have proof of implant safety.

Mercury in Dentistry

The FDA committee which was suppose to approve amalgam did not approve mixed dental amalgam. Their explanation was that the finished product (filling) is manufactured by individual dentists and therefore could not be approved.

It is safe to say that the burden of responsibility for material selection rests with the trained professional. The Supreme Court of Sweden ruled in a case of adverse patient reaction to dental materials that selection of proper materials is the individual dentist's responsibility and not the government's. If that responsibility is shirked or ignored, both the patient and dentists' reputation will suffer.

Dr. Vimy's research clearly indicates that the issue of dental filling safety is a medical issue, not a dental one. It is clear from the research that dental schools and dentists lack the necessary training or facilities to adequately evaluate dental materials. Replacement of non-biocompatible materials with more compatible materials is one viable option however that course is further complicated by the fact that the patient will be exposed to mercury during the removal unless the International Academy of Oral Medicine and Toxicology's *Patient Protection Protocols* are followed. Certainly, as a first step, As a first step the profession as a whole should immediately comply with the manufacturers MSDS recommendations and the further placement of toxic materials in children and pregnant women should cease immediately.

Whatever the outcome, failure to act prudently will surely diminish the value of this profession in the long run. Dentistry's long history of flagrant disregard for industrial exposure standards must end. Dentisty's 20-year failure to bring the dental offices into compliance with the present lenient law has resulted in injury to patients, dentists and dental staffs.

One can only speculate at this point as to why this failure has occurred. Certainly professional organizations and educational institutions must share a significant portion of the responsibility. In the years when I attended the University of Missouri at Kansas City from 1967 to 1971, the subject of mercury toxicity was never even mentioned. To this day, few of the facts reviewed in this presentation are common knowledge among dentists. New graduates are equally unfamiliar with the problems and issues discussed here. A colleague of mine in France writes, "It's not easy to speak about the problem of mercury in France." It has never been "easy" to reject conventional wisdom and follow the path dictated by science and

Mercury in Dentistry

knowledge. All that is required is detailed scientific knowledge, moral conviction, and the courage to be criticized by those who lack the former.

While this paper has focused primarily on mercury, it is important to point out that several other common dental materials should also be subjected to closer scrutiny. Many materials in use today have failed to pass even the most elementary biocompatibility testing. In my own practice I have meticulously attempted to remove all such agents from my office.

Dr. Max Planck developed the quantum theory of physics in 1901. Albert Einstein read Dr. Planck's theory and in 1905 used quantum physics to arrive at $E=mc^2$. Quantum physics has only recently become widely recognized as a valid scientific theory. After trying for years with only limited success to have his new concepts accepted by the "established scientific community," Dr. Planck was quoted as saying, *New ideas enter science not by old men considering new data and arriving at new conclusions, but by old men dying.*

It is true that a word to the wise is sufficient, but a fool you can tell a thousand times. Let us not become a profession of fools, but rather let us listen to the words of the scientific community. We should abandon materials which do not meet the highest biocompatibility standards or which increase the patient's body burden of toxins--for the safety of the patients, the families, and the staff.

[1]   Berlin MH, Nordberg GF, Serenius F. On the site and mechanism of mercury vapor resorption in the lung. Arch Environ Health 18: 42-50, 1969.

[2]   Clarkson TW, Magos L, Greenwood MR. The transport of elemental mercury into fetal tissues. Biol Neonate 21: 239-44, 1972.

[3]   Berlin M, Fazackerley J, Nordberg G. The uptake of mercury in the brains of mammals exposed to mercury vapor and to mercuric salts. Arch Environ Health 18: 719-29, 1969.

[4]   Ware RA, Chang LW, Burkholder PM. An ultrastructure study on the blood-brain barrier dysfunction following mercury intoxication. Acta Neuropathology (Berlin) 30: 211-24, 1974.

[5] Chang LW and Hartman HA. Blood-brain barrier dysfunction in experimental mercury intoxication. Acta Neuropathology 21: 179-84, 1972.

[6] Schaumberger HH, Spencer PS. Clinical and experimental studies of distal axonopathy--a frequent form of brain and nerve damage. Produced by Environmental Chemical Hazards. Annals of New York Academy of Science, Vol. 329: 14-29, 1979.

[7] Chang LW. Neurotoxic effects of mercury: a review. Environmental Research 14: 329-73, 1977.

[8] Gallagher PJ, Lee RL. The role of biotransformation in organic mercury neurotoxicity. Toxicology 15: 129-34, 1980.

[9] Clarkson TW. Biochemical aspects of mercury poisoning, Journal of Occupational Medicine 10: 351-55, July 1968.

[10] Gerstner HB, Huff JE. Clinical toxicology of mercury. Journal of Toxicology and Environmental Health, Vol. 2, Issue 3: 491-526, 1977.

[11] Stock A: Die gefahrlichkeit des quecksilberdampfes. Z Angew Chem 39: 461-88, 1926.

[12] Wedeen RP. Were the hatters of New Jersey "mad"? American Journal of Industrial Medicine 16: 255-33, 1989.

[13] Verschaeve L, et al., Genetic damage induced by occupational low mercury exposure. Environmental Research 12: 306-16, 1976.

[14] Skerfving S, Hansson K, and Linstren J. Chromosome breakage in humans exposed to methylmercury through fish consumption. Archives of Environmental Health 21: 133-39, 1970.

[15] Popescu HI, et al. Chromosome aberration induced by occupational exposure to mercury. Archives of Environmental Health Vol. 34, Issue 6: 461-63, 1979.

[16] Fiskesjo G. The effect of two organic mercury compounds on human leukocytes in vitro. Hereditas 64:142-46, 1970.

[17] Weening JJ, et al. Mercury induced immune complex glomerulopathy: an experimental study. Chapter 4: pp 36-66. VanDendergen, 1980.

[18] Weening JJ, et al. Autoimmune reactions and glomerulonephritis caused by heavy metals and other toxins. Dev Toxicol Environ Sci 11: 211-16, 1983.

[19] Koller LD, et al. Immuno response in rats supplemented with selenium. Clin Exp Immunol 63 (3): 570-76, 1986.

[20] Koller LD. Immunosuppression produced by lead, cadmium, mercury. Am J Vet Res 34: 1457-58, 1973.

[21] Koller LD. Immunotoxicology of heavy metals. International J immunopharmacology 2: 269-79, 1980.

[22] Koller LD. Methyl mercury: effect on oncogenic and nononcogenic viruses in mice. Am J Vet Res 36: 1501-04, 1975.

[23] Eggleston DW. Effect of dental amalgam and nickel alloys on T-lymphocytes: preliminary report. J Prosthet Dent 51: 617-23, 1984.

[24] Stejfkal V; Evaluating the Systemic Immune Response to Mercury Compounds International Academy of Oral Medicine and Toxicology Annual Scientific Session Seattle, Wash 9/1991

[25] Sharma RP, Obersteiner EJ. Metals and neurotoxic effects: cytotoxicity of selected metallic compounds on chick ganglia cultures. Journal of Comp. Pathology, Vol. 91, 1981.

[26] Environmental Health Criteria 118: Inorganic Mercury. World Health Organization, Geneva, 1991.

[27] Gay DD, Cox RD, Reinhardt JW. Chewing releases mercury from fillings. Corresp Lancet 1 (8123): 985-86, 1979.

[28] Svare CW et al. The effect of dental amalgams on mercury levels in expired air. J. Dent Res 1981 : 60 : 1668-71

[29] Reinhardt JW, et al. Exhaled mercury following removal and insertion of amalgam restorations. J Prosth Dent. 1983 : 49(5) : 652-6

[30] Cross JD, Dole IM, Goolvard L, Lenihan JMA, Smith H: Methyl mercury in the blood of dentists. (Corresp) Lancet 1978 2(8084) :312-3

[31] Svare CW, Peterson LC: The Effect of Removing Dental Amalgams on Mercury Blood Levels. J Dent Res 1984, 63: 896 (Abstract)

[32] Fredin B., Studies on the mercury released from dental amalgam fillings (1985) submitted for publication

[33] Patterson JE et al. Mercury in human breath from dental amalgams. Bull Envir Contam Toxicol 1985: 34 : 459-68

[34] Vimy MJ and Lorscheider FL. Intra-oral air mercury released from dental amalgam. J Dent Res 1985: 64(8) : 1069-71

Mercury in Dentistry

35   Vimy MJ and Lorscheider FL Serial measurements of intra-oral air mercury : Estimation of daily dose from dental amalgam. J Dent Res. 64 (8) : 1072-1075 , 1985b.

36   Patterson JE, Weisberg BG, Dennison JP,. Mercury in Human breath from dental amalgam. Bull Environ. Conatam. Toxicol. 34: 459-468, 1985

37   Vimy MJ, Luft AJ, Lorscheider FL. Estimation of Mercury Body Burden from Dental Amalgam Computer Simulation of a Metabolic Compartment Model. J. Dent. Res 1986 65(12):1415-1419, December, 1986

38   Abraham JE, Svare CW, Frank CW. The effect of dental amalgam restoration on blood mercury levels. J Dent Res 63(1): 71-3, 1984

39   Sellars R Jr. et al. Safety of Amalgam: Toxicity and Allergy Amalgam Survives Systemic Toxicity Challenge. Texas Dent J July, 1986

40   Personal communication with Rodney Sellars, Jr. D.D.S. Caldwell, TX 1991

41   Abraham op. cit.

42   Kroncke A. et al. Uber die guecksilberkonzentrationen in blut und urin von personen mit und ohne amalgemfullungen. Dtsch Zahnaerztl Z. 35:803-808, 1980

43   Ott K, and Kroncke A. Mercury concentrations in blood and urine of patients with or without amalgam fillings. J Dent Res. 60(13):1210, Abstract #48, 1981

44   Snapp K.R. Svare C.W. and Peterson L.D. Contribution of Dental Amalgams to Blood Mercury Levels. J Dent Res 65:311, Abstract #1276, Special issue

45   Till T and Maly K. Mercury in tooth roots and in Jaw bones ZRW 87 (6) : 288-2909 1978

46   Goldwater L, Ladd AC, Jacobs MB. Absorption and excretion of mercury in Man VII Significance of mercury in blood. Arch Environ Health 1964: 9:735-40.

47   Bernard SR. and Perdue P. (1934): Metabolic model for methyl and inorganic mercury. Health Physics 46: 695-699

48   Chang LW. 1977. op cit.

49   Stortebecker Mercury Poisoning from Dental Amalgam a Hazard to Human Brain ISBN 91-86034-05-7

50   Eggleston DW, Nylander M, Suffin SC, Martinoff JT, Rieders, MF. Correlation of dental amalgam with mercury in brain tissue. J Pros Dent 58:704-7, 1987

51   WHO Environmental Health Criteria 118: Inorganic Mercury. World Health Organization, Geneva, 1991

52   Freden H, Hellden L, Milleding P: Mercury content in gingival tissues adjacent to amalgam fillings. Odonto Rev 25:207-10, 1974

53   Clarkson TW, Friberg L, Hursh, J., and Nylander, M."Biological Monitoring of Toxic Metals" in Clarkson TW, Friberg L, Nordberg GF & Sager p: Eds. Plenum Press, N.Y. Feb 1988

54   Socialstyrelsen report May 20, 1987 as reported in Svenska Dagbladet. Bioprobe Vol 4 6/87 issue 3

55   Goldwater LJ: The toxicology of inorganic mercury. Annals NY Acad Sci 65:498-503, 1957

56   Goldwater LJ. Ladd AC. and Jacobs MB Absorption and Excretion of Mercury in Man; VII Significance of mercury in Blood. Arch Envir Health, 9:835-741: 1964

57   National Institute of Dental Research (NIDR) Workshop on the biocompatibility of metals in dentistry JADA (169-171) VOL109, 1984

58   Battistone GC, Hefferren JJ, Miller RA, Cutright DE: Mercury: its relation to the dentist's health and dental practice characteristics. J Amer Dent Assoc 92:1182-8, 1976

59   Abraham op cit. 1984

60   Daunderer M. Mobiliztation test for environmental mental poisonings Forum des Praktischen und Allgemedn-Arxtes 28(3):88, 1989

61   Langan DC, Fan PL, Hoos AA. The use of mercury in dentistry: a critical review of the recent literature. JADA 115:867-880, 1987

62   Berlin MH, Fazackerley J, Nordberg G: The uptake of mercury in the brains of mammals exposed to mercury vapor and to mercuric salts. Arch Environ Health 18:719-29, 1969.

63   Goldwater LJ. Ladd AC. and Jacobs MB Absorption and Excretion of Mercury in Man; VII Significance of mercury in Blood. Arch Envir Health, 9:835-741: 1964

64   Naleway C, Sakaguchi R, Mitchell E, Muller T, Ayer WA, Hefferren JJ: Urinary mercury levels in U.S. dentists, 1975-1983: review of health assessment. J Amer Dent Ass 111:37-42, 1985

65   Brown D: Detection of Mercury Vapor in Dental Surgery British Dental Journal Vol 155, 1983

66   Nixon GS, Rowbotham TC: Mercury hazards associated with high speed mechanical amalgamators. Brit Dent J 131:308-11, 1971

Mercury in Dentistry

67 Kantor L. et al. Mercury vapor in the dental office does carpeting make a difference. JADA 103(9):402-407, 1981

68 Chopp, G.F. & Kaufman EG. Mercury vapor related to manipulation of amalgam and to floor surface. Oper Dent 8(1):23-27, 1983

69 Cutright DE, Miller RA, Battistone GC, Millikan LJ: Systemic mercury levels caused by inhaling mist during high-speed amalgam grinding. J Oral Med 28:100-4, 1973

70 Gronka PA, Bobkoskie RL, Tomchick GJ, Back F, Rakow AB: Mercury vapor exposures in dental offices. J Amer Dent Assoc 81:923-5, 1970

71 Roydhous RH et al. Mercury in dental offices. J Can Dent 51(2):156-158, 1985

72 Mantyla DG, Wright OD: Mercury Toxicity in the dental office: a neglected problem. JADA 92:1189-94, 1976

73 Gordon HP, Gordon LD: Reduction in mercury vapor levels in Seattle dental offices. J Dent Res Abstract #1092 57A:347, 1978.

74 Schulein, TM, Reinhardt JW & Chan KC. Survey of Des Moines area dental offices for mercury Vapor. Iowa Dent J. 70(1):35-36, 1984

75 Ochoa, R & Miller R.W. Report on independent survey of American dental offices for mercury contamination. Tex Dent J. 100(1):6-9 1983

76 Stortebecker P. Direct Transport of Mercury from the Oronasal Cavity to the Cranial Cavity as a cause of Dental Amalgam Poisoning, Swed J. Biol Med 3/89

77 Stortebecker P. Mercury Poisoning from Dental Amalgam- A Hazard to the Human Brain. Stortebecker Foundation for Research, Stockholm, Sweden, 1985

78 Stock A: Die chronische Quecksilber-und Amalgamvergiftung. Arch Gewerbepath Gewerbehyg 1936, 7: 388-413.

79 Stock A. Der quecksilbergehalt des menschlichen Organismus II. XXXIII Mittellung Uber Wirkung und Verbreitung des Quecksilbers. Biochem Z 1943, 316 108-122

80 Gordon H. Pregnancy in female dentists - A mercury hazard. In proceedings of the International Conference on Mercury Hazards in Dental Practice Gloscow, Scotland 2-4 Sept 1981

81 Panova Z et al. Ovarian function in women having professional contact with mercury. Akusherstvoi Ginekologiya 13(1) : n29-34, 1974

82 Noe FE: Mercury as a potential hazard in medical laboratories. New Eng J Med 261:1002-6, 1959

83 Cook, T Yates P. Fatal mercury intoxication in a dental surgery assistant. British Dent J. 127(12):553-555, Dec 1969

84 Marinova G et al. A study of the reproductive function in women working with mercury. Problemi na akuserstvoto i Ginekologiyata 1:75-77, 1973

85 Sikorski R. et al. Women in dental surgeries: reproductive hazards in occupational exposure to metallic mercury. Int Arch Occup Environ Health. 59 (6):551-557, 1987

86 Gelbier S, Ingram J. Possible fetotoxic effects of mercury vapor: a case report. Public Health 103(1):35-40 1/1989

87 Brune, D.K.. Edling, C., Occupational Hazards in the Health Professions Chapter 16, 315-316 Boca Raton Fl: CRC Press, Inc, 1989

88 Koos BJ and Longo LD. Mercury Toxicity in the pregnant woman, fetus, and newborn infant. A review Am J Obstetrics and Gynocology 126(3):390-409, 1976

89 A.D.A. Council on Dental Materials and Devices: Recommendations in mercury hygiene. J Amer Dent Assoc 88:391-2, 1974

90 Langan DC, Fan PL, Hoos AA, The use of mercury in dentistry: a critical review of the recent literature. JADA 115:867-880, 1987

91 Cutright DE, Miller RA, Battistone GC, Millikan LJ: Systemic mercury levels caused by inhaling mist during high-speed amalgam grinding. J Oral Med 28:100-4, 1973

92 Eggleston DW. Dental Amalgam -- To Be or Not To Be Pacific Coast Society of Prosthodontists Newsletter 9(2):4-10 10,1989

93 Cook TA op. cit.

94 U.S.E.P.A. Mercury Health Effects Update. Final Report (1984)EPA-600/8-84-019F United States Environmental Protection Agency, Office of Health and Environment Assessment. Washington, D.C. 20460.

95 Verschoor MA, Herbert RFM, Zielhuis RL. Urinary Mercury Levels and Early Changes in Kidney Function in Dentists and Dental Assistants. Community Dentistry and Oral Epidemiology, Vol. 16 #3, June 1988.

96   Pitkin RM, Bahns JA, Filer LJ Jr, Reynolds WA. Mercury in human maternal and cord blood, placenta and milk. Soc Exper Biol Med Proc 1976: 151: 565-7.

97   Kuntz WD, Pitkin RM, Bostrom AW, Hughes MS: Maternal and Cord Blood Background Mercury Levels: a longitudinal surveillance. Am J Obstet Gynecol 143(4):440-3, 1982.

98   Vimy, M.J.; Takahashi, T.; Lorscheider, F.L. Maternal-Fetal Distribution of Mercury (203 Hg) Released from Dental Amalgam Fillings. Journal of American Physiological Society, April 1990

99   Berlin, M Hua, J Logdberg, and Warvinge University of Lund, Institute of Environmental Medicine, Lund Sweden (Abstract The Toxicologist 31st Annual Meeting Vol 12 #1 February 1992)

100 Mikhailova LM et al. The influence of occupational factors on disease of the female reproductive organs. Pediatriya Akusherstvoi Ginekologiya. 33(6)56-58, 1971

101 Panova Z and Dimitrov G, Ovarian function in women having professional contact with metallic mercury. Akusherstvoi Ginekologiya 13(1):29-34, 1974

102 Goncharuk GA, Problems relating to occupational hygiene of women in production of mercury. Gigiena Truda i Professional nye Zabolevaniya. 5:17-20, 1977

103 Rowland A, Baird D, Weinberg C, Shore D Shy C and Wilcox A Reduced Fertility Among Dental Assistants With Occupational Exposure to Mercury; National Institute of Environmental Health Sciences, Research Triangle, NC (Abstract The Toxicologist 31st Annual Meeting Vol 12 #1 February 1992)

104 Yang S. Influence of lead on female reproductive function. Chung Hua Fu Chan Ko Tsa Chih, 21(4):208-210, Jun 1986 (English abstract p 252)

105 Koos BJ and Longo LD. Mercury Toxicity in the pregnant woman, fetus, and newborn infant. A review Am J Obstetrics and Gynecology 126(3):390-409, 1976

106 Berlin op cit.

107 Dencker et al.,University of Uppsala (Abstract The Toxicologist 31st Annual Meeting Vol 12 #1 February 1992)

108 Pierce P et al. Alkyl mercury poisoning in humans. Report of an outbreak. JAMA 220:1439-1442, 1972

109 Snyder RD. Congenital mercury poisoning. N Eng J Med. 18:1014-1016, 1971

110 Council on Dental Materials, Instruments, and Equipment (CDMIE) Instructions for handling dental amalgam a toxic substance, ADA Journal 10/84 (Vol. 109:617-9)

111 U.S. OSHA Dental Amalgam a toxic hazard Material Safety Data Sheet (MSDS). ADA News 1 Aug 1988 [19(15):1.]

112 EPA Dental Amalgam a Toxic Hazard ADA News 20(2):1,6 16 Jan 1989

113 JADA, Special Report: When your patients ask about mercury in amalgam. Vol 120, p 395-398 April 1990

114 Bass MH: Idiosyncrasy to metallic mercury, with special reference to amalgam fillings in the teeth. J Pediat 23:215-8, 1943

115 Johnson HH, Schenberg IL, Bach NF: Chronic atrophic dermatitis, with pronounced mercury sensitivity: partial clearing after extraction of teeth containing mercury amalgam fillings. Arch Dermatol Syph 63:279, 1951

116 Feuerman E: Dermatitis due to mercury in amalgam dental fillings. Contact Dermatitis 1:191, 1975

117 Feuerman EJ: Recurrent contact dermatitis caused by mercury in amalgam dental fillings. Intern'l J Dermatol 14:657-60, 1975

118 Nakayama H, Niki F, Shono M, Hada S: Mercury exanthem. Contact Dermatitis 9(5) 411-7, 1983.

119 Swinyer LJ: Allergic contact dermatitis from metallic mercury. Contact Dermatitis 6(3):226-7, 1980

120 Fernstrom AIB, Frkholm KO, Huldt S: Mercury allergy with eczematous dermatitis due to silver amalgam fillings. Br Dent J 113:204-6, 1962

121 Bergenholtz A: Multiple polypous hyperplasias of the oral mucosa with regression after removal of amalgam fillings. Acta Odon Scand 23:111-31, 1965

122 Engelman MA: Mercury allergy resulting from amalgam restorations. J Amer Dent Assoc 66:122-3, 1963

123 Hanzely B, Hadhazy S. Allergic reaction elicited by amalgam filling. Fogorv Szeml 73:208-9, 1980

124 Spector LA. Allergic manifestation to mercury. J Amer Dent Assoc 42:320, 1951

125 Catsakis LH, Sulica VI. Allergy to silver amalgams. Oral Surg 46:371-5, 1978

126 Frykholm KO, Frithiof L, Fernstrom AIB, Moberger G, Blohm SG, Bjorn E. Allergy to copper derived from dental alloys as a possible cause of oral lesions of lichen planus. Acta Derm Venereol 49:268-81, 1969

127 Lundstrom IMC: Allergy and corrosion of dental materials in patients with oral lichen planus. Int J Oral Surg 13:16-24, 1984.

[128] Mobacken H, Hersle K, Sloberg K, Thilander H. Oral lichen planus: hypersensitivity to dental restoration material. Contact Dermatitis 10(1) 11-5, 1984

[129] Finne K. et al. Oral Lichen planus and contact allergy to mercury. International Journal of Oral Surgery, Vol. 10:11-15, 1984

[130] Jolly M, Moule AJ, Freeman S. Amalgam-related chronic ulceration of oral mucosa. Br Dent J 160:434-7, 1986.

[131] James J, Ferguson MM, Forsyth A. Mercury allergy as a cause of burning mouth. Br Dent J 159:392, 1985

[132] White RR, Brandt RL. Development of mercury hypersensitivity among dental students. J Amer Dent Assoc 92:1204-7, 1976

[133] Miller EG, Perry WL, Wagner MJ. Prevalence of mercury hypersensitivity in dental students. J Dent Res 64:(Spec Issue Abstracts) Abstract 1472, page 338, March, 1985.

[134] Djerassi E. and Berova N. The possibilities of allergic reaction from silver amalgam restorations. Int Dent J. 19 (4) : 481-488, 1969

[135] Neuman Sheldon, D.D.S. California Dental Association Scientific Session, Anaheim, Ca. U.S.A. May, 1987

[136] Julin L, Ohman S: Allergic reaction to mercury in red tattoos and in mucosa adjacent to amalgam fillings. Acta Derm Venereol 48:103-5, 1968

[137] Contact dermatitis in dentists and hospital personnel wearing gloves Journal of Michigan Dental Association 4/1990

[138] Shapiro IM, Sumner AJ, Spitz LK, Cornblath DR, Uzzell B, Ship II, Bloch P. Neurophysiological and neuropsychological function in mercury-exposed dentists. Lancet 8282:1147-50, 1982

[139] Nylander M. Mercury in pituitary glands of dentists. Lancet 442, Feb 22, 1986

[140] Friberg L, Kullman L, Lind B, Nylander M. Kvicksilver i centrala nervsystemet i relation till amalgamfyllningar (Mercury in the central nervous system in relation to dental amalgam). Lakartidningen 83:519-22, 1986.

[141] Ahlbom, A., Norell, S., Rodvall, Y., and Nylander, M. Dentists, dental nurses, and brain tumors, Br. Med. J., 292, 662, 1986

MATERIAL SAFETY DATA SHEET DISPERSALLOY® DISPERSED PHASE ALLOY Tablets powder and Capsules Dentsply Caulk 38 West Clarke Avenue
Milford DE 19963-0359 Phone (302) 422-4511 9/20/95 Dated Revised 9/24/97